The Telegraph Girl

Anthony Trollope

Kessinger Publishing's Rare Reprints

Thousands of Scarce and Hard-to-Find Books on These and other Subjects!

- Americana
- Ancient Mysteries
- Animals
- Anthropology
- Architecture
- Arts
- Astrology
- Bibliographies
- Biographies & Memoirs
- Body, Mind & Spirit
- Business & Investing
- Children & Young Adult
- Collectibles
- Comparative Religions
- Crafts & Hobbies
- Earth Sciences
- Education
- Ephemera
- Fiction
- Folklore
- Geography
- Health & Diet
- History
- Hobbies & Leisure
- Humor
- Illustrated Books
- Language & Culture
- Law
- Life Sciences

- Literature
- Medicine & Pharmacy
- Metaphysical
- Music
- Mystery & Crime
- Mythology
- Natural History
- Outdoor & Nature
- Philosophy
- Poetry
- Political Science
- Science
- Psychiatry & Psychology
- Reference
- Religion & Spiritualism
- Rhetoric
- Sacred Books
- Science Fiction
- Science & Technology
- Self-Help
- Social Sciences
- Symbolism
- Theatre & Drama
- Theology
- Travel & Explorations
- War & Military
- Women
- Yoga
- *Plus Much More!*

We kindly invite you to view our catalog list at:
http://www.kessinger.net

THE TELEGRAPH GIRL.

CHAPTER I.

LUCY GRAHAM AND SOPHY WILSON.

THREE shillings a day to cover all expenses of life, food, raiment, shelter, a room in which to eat and sleep, and fire and light,—and recreation if recreation there might be,—is not much; but when Lucy Graham, the heroine of this tale, found herself alone in the world, she was glad to think that she was able to earn so much by her work, and that thus she possessed the means of independence if she chose to be independent. Her story up to the date with which we are dealing shall be very shortly told. She had lived for many years with a married brother, who was a bookseller in Holborn,—in a small way of business, and burdened with a large family, but still living in decent comfort. In order, however, that she might earn her own bread she had gone into the service of the Crown as a "Telegraph Girl" in the Telegraph Office.* And there

* I presume my readers to be generally aware that the head-quarters of the National Telegraph Department are held at the top of one of the great buildings belonging to the General Post Office, in St. Martin's-le-Grand.

she had remained till the present time, and there
she was earning eighteen shillings a week by eight
hours' continual work daily. Her life had been full of
occupation, as in her spare hours she had been her
brother's assistant in his shop, and had made herself
familiar with the details of his trade. But the brother
had suddenly died, and it had been quickly decided
that the widow and the children should take themselves off to some provincial refuge.

Then it was that Lucy Graham had to think of her
independence and her eighteen shillings a week on the
one side, and of her desolation and feminine necessities
on the other. To run backwards and forwards from
High Holborn to St. Martin's-le-Grand had been very
well as long as she could comfort herself with the
companionship of her sister-in-law and defend herself
with her brother's arm;—but how would it be with her
if she were called upon to live all alone in London?
She was driven to consider what else she could do to
earn her bread. She might become a nursemaid, or
perhaps a nursery governess. Though she had been
well and in some respects carefully educated, she knew
that she could not soar above that. Of music she did
not know a note. She could draw a little and understood
enough French,—not to read it, but to teach herself
to read it. With English literature she was better
acquainted than is usual with young women of her age
and class; and, as her only personal treasures, she had
managed to save a few books which had become hers
through her brother's kindness. To be a servant was
distasteful to her, not through any idea that service
was disreputable, but from a dislike to be subject at
all hours to the will of others. To work and work

hard she was quite willing, so that there might be some hours of her life in which she might not be called upon to obey.

When, therefore, it was suggested to her that she had better abandon the Telegraph Office and seek the security of some household, her spirit rebelled against the counsel. Why should she not be independent, and respectable, and safe? But then the solitude! Solitude would certainly be hard, but absolute solitude might not perhaps be necessary. She was fond too of the idea of being a government servant, with a sure and fixed salary,—bound of course to her work at certain hours, but so bound only for certain hours. During a third of the day she was, as she proudly told herself, a servant of the Crown. During the other two-thirds she was lord,—or lady,—of herself.

But there was a quaintness, a mystery, even an awe, about her independence which almost terrified her. During her labours she had eight hundred female companions, all congregated together in one vast room, but as soon as she left the Post Office she was to be all alone! For a few months after her brother's death she continued to live with her sister-in-law, during which time this great question was being discussed. But then the sister-in-law and the children disappeared, and it was incumbent on Lucy to fix herself somewhere. She must begin life after what seemed to her to be a most unfeminine fashion,—"just as though she were a young man,"—for it was thus that she described to herself her own position over and over again.

At this time Lucy Graham was twenty-six years old. She had hitherto regarded herself as being stronger and more steadfast than are women generally of that age. She had taught herself to despise feminine weaknesses, and had learned to be almost her brother's equal in managing the affairs of his shop in his absence. She had declared to herself, looking forward then to some future necessity which had become present to her with terrible quickness, that she would not be feckless, helpless, and insufficient for herself as are so many females. She had girded herself up for a work-a-day life,—looking forward to a time when she might leave the telegraphs and become a partner with her brother. A sudden disruption had broken up all that.

She was twenty-six, well made, cheery, healthy, and to some eyes singularly good-looking, though no one probably would have called her either pretty or handsome. In the first place her complexion was—brown. It was impossible to deny that her whole face was brown, as also was her hair, aud generally her dress. There was a pervading brownness about her which left upon those who met her a lasting connection between Lucy Graham and that serviceable, long-enduring colour. But there was nobody so convinced that she was brown from head to foot as was she herself. A good lasting colour she would call it,—one that did not require to be washed every half-hour in order that it might be decent, but could bear real washing when it was wanted; for it was a point of her inner creed, of her very faith of faith, that she was not to depend upon feminine good looks, or any of the adventitious charms of dress for her advance in the world. "A good strong binding," she would say of certain dark-visaged books, "that will stand the gas, and not look disfigured even though a blot of ink should come in its way."

And so it was that she regarded her own personal binding.

But for all that she was to some observers very attractive. There was not a mean feature in her face. Her forehead was spacious and well formed. Her eyes, which were brown also, were very bright, and could sparkle with anger or solicitude, or perhaps with love. Her nose was well formed, and delicately shaped enough. Her mouth was large, but full of expression, and seemed to declare without speech that she could be eloquent. The form of her face was oval, and complete, not as though it had been moulded by an inartistic thumb, a bit added on here and a bit there. She was somewhat above the average height of women, and stood upon her legs,—or walked upon them,—as though she understood that they had been given to her for real use.

Two years before her brother's death there had been a suitor for her hand,—as to whose suit she had in truth doubted much. He also had been a bookseller, a man in a larger way of business than her brother, some fifteen years older than herself,—a widower, with a family. She knew him to be a good man, with a comfortable house, an adequate income, and a kind heart. Had she gone to him she would not have been required then to live among the bookshelves or the telegraphs. She had doubted much whether she would not go to him. She knew she could love the children. She thought that she could buckle herself to that new work with a will. But she feared,—she feared that she could not love him.

Perhaps there had come across her heart some idea of what might be the joy of real, downright, hearty

love. If so it was only an idea. No personage had
come across her path thus to disturb her. But the
idea, or the fear, had been so strong with her that she
had never been able to induce herself to become the
wife of this man; and when he had come to her after
her brother's death, in her worst desolation,—when the
prospect of service in some other nursery had been
strongest before her eyes,—she had still refused him.
Perhaps there had been a pride in this,—a feeling that
as she had rejected him in her comparative prosperity,
she should not take him now when the renewal of his
offer might probably be the effect of generosity. But
she did refuse him; and the widowed bookseller had
to look elsewhere for a second mother for his children.

Then there arose the question, how and where she
should live? When it came to the point of settling
herself, that idea of starting in life like a young man
became very awful indeed. How was she to do it?
Would any respectable keeper of lodgings take her in
upon that principle? And if so, in what way should
she plan out her life? Sixteen hours a day were to be
her own. What should she do with them? Was she
or was she not to contemplate the enjoyment of any
social pleasures; and if so, how were they to be found
of such a nature as not to be discreditable? On rare
occasions she had gone to the play with her brother,
and had then enjoyed the treat thoroughly. Whether
it had been *Hamlet* at the Lyceum, or *Lord Dundreary*
at the Haymarket, she had found herself equally able
to be happy. But there could not be for her now even
such rare occasions as these. She thought that she
knew that a young woman all alone could not go to
the theatre with propriety, let her be ever so brave.

And then those three shillings a day, though sufficient for life, would hardly be more than sufficient.

But how should she begin? At last chance assisted her. Another girl, also employed in the Telegraph Office, with whom there had been some family acquaintance over and beyond that formed in the office, happened at this time to be thrown upon the world in some such fashion as herself and the two agreed to join their forces.

She was one Sophy Wilson by name,—and it was agreed between them that they should club their means together and hire a room for their joint use. Here would be a companionship,—and possibly, after awhile, sweet friendship. Sophy was younger than herself, and might probably need, perhaps be willing to accept, assistance. To be able to do something that should be of use to somebody would, she felt, go far towards giving her life that interest which it would otherwise lack.

When Lucy examined her friend, thinking of the closeness of their future connection, she was startled by the girl's prettiness and youth, and thorough unlikeness to herself. Sophy had long, black, glossy curls, large eyes, a pink complexion, and was very short. She seemed to have no inclination for that strong, serviceable brown binding which was so valuable in Lucy's eyes; but rather to be wedded to bright colours and soft materials. And it soon became evident to the elder young woman that the younger looked upon her employment simply as a stepping-stone to a husband. To get herself married as soon as possible was unblushingly declared by Sophy Wilson to be the one object of her ambition,—and as she supposed that of every other girl in the telegraph department. But she seemed to be friendly and at first docile, to have been brought up with aptitudes for decent life, and to be imbued with the necessity of not spending more than her three shillings a day. And she was quick enough at her work in the office,—quicker even than Lucy herself,—which was taken by Lucy as evidence that her new friend was clever, and would therefore probably be an agreeable companion.

They took together a bedroom in a very quiet street in Clerkenwell,—a street which might be described as genteel because it contained no shops; and here they began to keep house, as they called it. Now the nature of their work was such that they were not called upon to be in their office till noon, but that then they were required to remain there till eight in the evening. At two a short space was allowed them for dinner, which was furnished to them at a cheap rate in a room adjacent to that in which they worked. Here for eightpence each they could get a good meal, or if they preferred it they could bring their food with them, and even have it cooked upon the premises. In the evening tea and bread and butter were provided for them by the officials; and then at eight or a few minutes after they left the building and walked home. The keeping of house was restricted in fact to providing tea and bread and butter for the morning meal, and perhaps when they could afford it for the repetition of such comfort later in the evening. There was the Sunday to be considered,—as to which day they made a contract with the keeper of the lodging-house to sit at her table and partake of her dishes. And so they were established.

From the first Lucy Graham made up her mind that it was her duty to be a very friend of friends to this new companion. It was as though she had consented to marry that widowed bookseller. She would then have considered herself bound to devote herself to his welfare. It was not that she could as yet say that she loved Sophy Wilson. Love with her could not be so immediate as that. But the nature of the bond between them was such, that each might possibly do so much either for the happiness, or the unhappiness of the other! And then, though Sophy was clever, —for as to this Lucy did not doubt,—still she was too evidently in many things inferior to herself, and much in want of such assistance as a stronger nature could give her. Lucy in acknowledging this put down her own greater strength to the score of her years and the nature of the life which she had been called upon to lead. She had early in her days been required to help herself, to hold her own, and to be as it were a woman of business. But the weakness of the other was very apparent to her. That doctrine as to the necessity of a husband, which had been very soon declared, had,—well,—almost disgusted Lucy. And then she found cause to lament the peculiar arrangement which the requirements of the office had made as to their hours. At first it had seemed to her to be very pleasant that they should have their morning hours for needlework, and perhaps for a little reading; but when she found that Sophy would lie in bed till ten because early rising was not obligatory, then she wished that they had been classed among those whose presence was demanded at eight.

After awhile, there was a little difference between

them as to what might or what might not be done
with propriety after their office hours were over. It
must be explained that in that huge room in which
eight hundred girls were at work together, there was
also a sprinkling of boys and young men. As no girls
were employed there after eight there would always
be on duty in the afternoon an increasing number of
the other sex, some of whom remained there till late
at night,—some indeed all night. Now, whether by
chance,—or as Lucy feared by management,—Sophy
Wilson had her usual seat next to a young lad with
whom she soon contracted a certain amount of intimacy. And from this intimacy arose a proposition
that they two should go with Mr. Murray,—he was at
first called Mister, but the formal appellation soon
degenerated into a familiar Alec,—to a Music Hall!
Lucy Graham at once set her face against the Music
Hall.

"But why?" asked the other girl. "You don't
mean to say that decent people don't go to Music
Halls?"

"I don't mean to say anything of the kind, but
then they go decently attended."

"How decently? We should be decent."

"With their brothers," said Lucy;—"or something
of that kind."

"Brothers!" ejaculated the other girl with a tone
of thorough contempt. A visit to a Music Hall with
her brother was not at all the sort of pleasure to which
Sophy was looking forward. She did her best to get
over objections which to her seemed to be fastidious
and absurd, observing, "that if people were to feel
like that there would be no coming together of people

at all." But when she found that Lucy could not be instigated to go to the Music Hall, and that the idea of Alec Murray and herself going to such a place unattended by others was regarded as a proposition too monstrous to be discussed, Sophy for awhile gave way. But she returned again and again to the subject, thinking to prevail by asserting that Alec had a friend, a most excellent young man, who would go with them, —and bring his sister. Alec was almost sure that the sister would come. Lucy, however, would have nothing to do with it. Lucy thought that there should be very great intimacy indeed before anything of that kind should be permitted.

And so there was something of a quarrel. Sophy declared that such a life as theirs was too hard for her, and that some kind of amusement was necessary. Unless she were allowed some delight she must go mad, she must die, she must throw herself off Waterloo Bridge. Lucy, remembering her duty, remembering how imperative it was that she should endeavour to do good to the one human being with whom she was closely concerned, forgave her, and tried to comfort her;—forgave her even though at last she refused to be guided by her monitress. For Sophy did go to the Music Hall with Alec Murray,—reporting, but reporting falsely, that they were accompanied by the friend and the friend's sister. Lucy, poor Lucy, was constrained by certain circumstances to disbelieve this false assertion. She feared that Sophy had gone with Alec alone,—as was the fact. But yet she forgave her friend. How are we to live together at all if we cannot forgive each other's offences?

CHAPTER II.

ABRAHAM HALL.

As there was no immediate repetition of the offence the forgiveness soon became complete, and Lucy found the interest of her life in her endeavours to be good to this weak child whom chance had thrown in her way. For Sophy Wilson was but a weak child. She was full of Alec Murray for awhile, and induced Lucy to make the young man's acquaintance. The lad was earning twelve shillings a week, and if these two poor young creatures chose to love each other and get themselves married, it would be respectable, though it might be unfortunate. It would at any rate be the way of the world, and was a natural combination with which she would have no right to interfere. But she found that Alec was a mere boy, and with no idea beyond the enjoyment of a bright scarf and a penny cigar, with a girl by his side at a Music Hall. "I don't think it can be worth your while to go much out of your way for his sake," said Lucy.

"Who is going out of her way? Not I. He's as good as anybody else, I suppose. And one must have somebody to talk to sometimes." These last words she uttered so plaintively, showing so plainly that she was unable to endure the simple unchanging dulness of a life of labour, that Lucy's heart was thoroughly softened towards her. She had the great gift of being not the less able to sympathize with the weakness of the weak because of her own abnormal strength. And so it came to pass that she worked for her friend,— stitching and mending when the girl ought to have stitched and mended for herself,—reading to her, even though but little of what was read might be understood,—yielding to her and assisting her in all things, till at last it came to pass that in truth she loved her. And such love and care were much wanted, for the elder girl soon found that the younger was weak in health as well as weak in spirit. There were days on which she could not,—or at any rate did not go to her office. When six months had passed by Lucy had not once been absent since she had begun her new life.

"Have you seen that man who has come to look at our house?" asked Sophy one day as they were walking down to the office. Lucy had seen a strange man, having met him on the stairs. "Isn't he a fine fellow?"

"For anything that I know. Let us hope that he is very fine," said Lucy laughing.

"He's about as handsome a chap as I think I ever saw."

"As for being a chap the man I saw must be near forty."

"He is a little old I should say, but not near that. I don't think he can have a wife or he wouldn't come here. He's an engineer, and he has the care of a steam-engine in the City Road, that great printing place. His name is Abraham Hall, and he's earning three or four pounds a week. A man like that ought to have a wife."

"How did you learn all about him?"

"It's all true. Sally heard it from Mrs. Green." Mrs. Green was the keeper of the lodging-house and Sally was the maid. "I couldn't help speaking to him yesterday because we were both at the door together.

He talked just like a gentleman although he was all smutty and greasy."

"I am glad he talked like a gentleman."

"I told him we lodged here and that we were telegraph girls, and that we never got home till half-past eight. He would be just the beau for you because he is such a big steady-looking fellow."

"I don't want a beau," said Lucy angrily.

"Then I shall take him myself," said Sophy as she entered the office.

Soon after that it came to pass that there did arise a slight acquaintance between both the girls and Abraham Hall, partly from the fact of their near neighbourhood, partly perhaps from some little tricks on Sophy's part. But the man seemed to be so steady, so solid, so little given to lightnesses of flirtation or to dangerous delights, that Lucy was inclined to welcome the accident. When she saw him on a Sunday morning free from the soil of his work, she could perceive that he was still a young man, probably not much over thirty;—but there was a look about him as though he were well inured to the cares of the world, such as is often produced by the possession of a wife and family, —not a look of depression by any means, but seeming to betoken an appreciation of the seriousness of life. From all this Lucy unconsciously accepted an idea of security in the man, feeling that it might be pleasant to have some strong one near her, from whom in case of need assistance might be asked without fear. For this man was tall and broad and powerful, and seemed to Lucy's eyes to be a very pillar of strength when he would stand still for a moment to greet her in the streets.

But poor Sophy, who had so graciously offered the man to her friend at the beginning of their intercourse, seemed soon to change her mind and to desire his attention for herself. He was certainly much more worthy than Alec Murray. But to Lucy, to whom it was a rule of life as strong as any in the commandments that a girl should not throw herself at a man, but should be sought by him, it was a painful thing to see how many of poor Sophy's much-needed sixpences were now spent in little articles of finery by which it was hoped that Mr. Hall's eyes might be gratified, and how those glossy ringlets were brushed and made to shine with pomatum, and how the little collars were washed and re-washed and starched and re-starched, in order that she might be smart for him. Lucy, who was always neat, endeavoured to become browner and browner. This she did by way of reproach and condemnation, not at all surmising that Mr. Hall might possibly prefer a good solid wearing colour to glittering blue and pink gewgaws.

At this time Sophy was always full of what Mr. Hall had last said to her; and after awhile broached an idea that he was some gentleman in disguise. "Why in disguise? Why not a gentleman not in disguise?" asked Lucy, who had her own ideas, perhaps a little exaggerated, as to Nature's gentlemen. Then Sophy explained herself. A gentleman, a real gentleman, in disguise would be very interesting;— one who had quarrelled with his father, perhaps, because he would not endure paternal tyranny, and had then determined to earn his own bread till he might happily come into the family honours and property in a year or two. Perhaps instead of being Abraham

Hall he was in reality the Right Honourable Russell Howard Cavendish; and if, during his temporary abeyance, he should prove his thorough emancipation from the thraldom of his aristocracy by falling in love with a telegraph girl, how fine it would be! When Lucy expressed an opinion that Mr. Hall might be a very fine fellow though he were fulfilling no more than the normal condition of his life at the present moment, Sophy would not be contented, declaring that her friend, with all her reading, knew nothing of poetry. In this way they talked very frequently about Abraham Hall, till Lucy would often feel that such talking was indecorous. Then she would be silent for awhile herself, and rebuke the other girl for her constant mention of the man's name. Then again she would be brought back to the subject;—for in all the little intercourse which took place between them and the man, his conduct was so simple and yet so civil, that she could not really feel him to be unworthy of a place in her thoughts. But Sophy soon declared frankly to her friend that she was absolutely in love with the man. "You wouldn't have him, you know," she said when Lucy scolded her for the avowal.

"Have him! How can you bring yourself to talk in such a way about a man? What does he want of either of us?"

"Men do marry you know,—sometimes," said Sophy; "and I don't know how a young man is to get a wife unless some girl will show that she is fond of him."

"He should show first that he is fond of her."

"That's all very well for talkee-talkee," said Sophy; "but it doesn't do for practice. Men are awfully shy. And then though they do marry sometimes, they don't want to get married particularly,—not as we do. It comes like an accident. But how is a man to fall into a pit if there's no pit open?"

In answer to this Lucy used many arguments and much scolding. But to very little effect. That the other girl should have thought so much about it and be so ready with her arguments was horrid to her. "A pit open!" ejaculated Lucy; "I would rather never speak to a man again than regard myself in such a light." Sophy said that all that might be very well, but declared that it "would not wash."

The elder girl was so much shocked by all this that there came upon her gradually a feeling of doubt whether their joint life could be continued. Sophy declared her purpose openly of entrapping Abraham Hall into a marriage, and had absolutely induced him to take her to the theatre. He had asked Lucy to join them; but she had sternly refused, basing her refusal on her inability to bear the expense. When he offered to give her the treat, she told him with simple gravity that nothing would induce her to accept such a favour from any man who was not either a very old friend or a near relation. When she said this he so looked at her that she was sure that he approved of her resolve. He did not say a word to press her;—but he took Sophy Wilson, and, as Lucy knew, paid for Sophy's ticket.

All this displeased Lucy so much that she began to think whether there must not be a separation. She could not continue to live on terms of affectionate friendship with a girl whose conduct she so strongly disapproved. But then again, though she could not restrain the poor light thing altogether, she did restrain her in some degree. She was doing some good by her companionship. And then, if it really was in the man's mind to marry the girl, that certainly would be a good thing,—for the girl. With such a husband she would be steady enough. She was quite sure that the idea of preparing a pit for such a one as Araham Hall must be absurd. But Sophy was pretty and clever, and if married would at any rate love her husband. Lucy thought she had heard that steady, severe, thoughtful men were apt to attach themselves to women of the butterfly order. She did not like the way in which Sophy was doing this; but then, who was she that she should be a judge? If Abraham Hall liked it, would not that be much more to the purpose? Therefore she resolved that there should be no separation at present;—and, if possible, no quarrelling.

But soon it came to pass that there was another very solid reason against separation. Sophy, who was often unwell, and would sometimes stay away from the office for a day or two on the score of ill-health, though by doing so she lost one of her three shillings on each such day, gradually became worse. The superintendent at her department had declared that in case of further absence a medical certificate must be sent, and the doctor attached to the office had called upon her. He had looked grave, had declared that she wanted considerable care, had then gone so far as to recommend rest,—which meant absence from work,—for at least a fortnight, and ordered her medicine. This of course meant the loss of a third of her wages. In such circumstances and at such a time it was not likely that Lucy should think of separation.

While Sophy was ill Abraham Hall often came to the door to inquire after her health;—so often that Lucy almost thought that her friend had succeeded. The man seemed to be sympathetic and anxious, and would hardly have inquired with so much solicitude had he not really been anxious as to poor Sophy's health. Then, when Sophy was better, he would come in to see her, and the girl would deck herself out with some little ribbon and would have her collar always starched and ironed, ready for his reception. It certainly did seem to Lucy that the man was becoming fond of her foolish little friend.

During this period Lucy of course had to go to the office alone, leaving Sophy to the care of the lodging-house keeper. And, in her solitude, troubles were heavy on her. In the first place Sophy's illness had created certain necessarily increased expenses; and at the same time their joint incomes had been diminished by one shilling a week out of six. Lucy was in general matters allowed to be the dispenser of the money; but on occasions the other girl would assert her rights,— which always meant her right to some indulgence out of their joint incomes which would be an indulgence to her and her alone. Even those bright ribbons could not be had for nothing. Lucy wanted no bright ribbons. When they were fairly prosperous she had not grudged some little expenditure in this direction. She had told herself that young girls like to be bright in the eyes of men, and that she had no right even to endeavour to make her friend look at all these things with her eyes. She even confessed to herself some deficiency on her own part, some want of womanliness in that she did not aspire to be attractive,—still owning to herself, vehemently declaring to herself, that to be attractive in the eyes of a man whom she could love would of all delights be the most delightful. Thinking of all this she had endeavoured not to be angry with poor Sophy; but when she became pinched for shillings and sixpences and to feel doubtful whether at the end of each fortnight there would be money to pay Mrs. Green for lodgings and coal, then her heart became sad within her, and she told herself that Sophy, though she was ill, ought to be more careful.

And there was another trouble which for awhile was very grievous. Telegraphy is an art not yet perfected among us and is still subject to many changes. Now it was the case at this time that the pundits of the office were in favour of a system of communicating messages by ear instead of by eye. The little dots and pricks which even in Lucy's time had been changed more than once, had quickly become familiar to her. No one could read and use her telegraphic literature more rapidly or correctly than Lucy Graham. But now that this system of little tinkling sounds was coming up,—a system which seemed to be very pleasant to those females who were gifted with musical aptitudes, —she found herself to be less quick, less expert, less useful than her neighbours. This was very sad, for she had always been buoyed up by an unconscious conviction of her own superior intelligence. And then, though there had been neither promises nor threats, she had become aware,—at any rate had thought that she was aware,—that those girls who could catch and use the tinkling sounds would rise more quickly to higher pay than the less gifted ones. She had struggled therefore to overcome the difficulty. She had endeavoured to force her ears to do that which her ears were not capable of accomplishing. She had failed, and to-day had owned to herself that she must fail. But Sophy had been one of the first to catch the tinkling sounds. Lucy came back to her room sad and down at heart and full of troubles. She had a long task of needle-work before her, which had been put by for awhile through causes consequent on Sophy's illness. "Now she is better perhaps he will marry her and take her away, and I shall be alone again," she said to herself, as though declaring that such a state of things would be a relief to her, and almost a happiness.

"He has just been here," said Sophy to her as soon as she entered the room. Sophy was painfully, cruelly smart, clean and starched, and shining about her locks,—so prepared that, as Lucy thought, she must have evidently expected him.

"Well;—and what did he say?"

"He has not said much yet, but it was very good of him to come and see me,—and he was looking so handsome. He is going out somewhere this evening to some political meeting with two or three other men, and he was got up quite like a gentleman. I do like to see him look like that."

"I always think a working man looks best in his working clothes," said Lucy. "There's some truth about him then. When he gets into a black coat he is pretending to be something else, but everybody can see the difference."

There was a severity, almost a savageness in this, which surprised Sophy so much that at first she hardly knew how to answer it. "He is going to speak at the meeting," she said after a pause. "And of course he had to make himself tidy. He told me all that he is going to say. Should you not like to hear him speak?"

"No," said Lucy very sharply; setting to work instantly upon her labours, not giving herself a moment for preparation or a moment for rest. Why should she like to hear a man speak who could condescend to love so empty and so vain a thing as that? Then she became gradually ashamed of her own feelings. "Yes," she said; "I think I should like to hear him speak;—only if I were not quite so tired. Mr. Hall is a man of good sense, and well educated, and I think I should like to hear him speak."

"I should like to hear him say one thing I know," said Sophy. Then Lucy in her rage tore asunder some fragment of a garment on which she was working.

CHAPTER III.
SOPHY WILSON GOES TO HASTINGS.

SOPHY went back to her work, and in a very few days was permanently moved from the seat which she had hitherto occupied next to Alec Murray and near to Lucy, to a distant part of the chamber in which the tinkling instruments were used. And as a part of the arrangement consequent on this she was called on to attend from ten till six instead of from noon till eight. And her hour for dining was changed also. In this way a great separation between the girls was made, for neither could they walk to the office together, nor walk from it. To Lucy, though she was sometimes inclined to be angry with her friend, this was very painful. But Sophy triumphed in it greatly. "I think we are to have a step up to 21*s.* in the musical box," she said laughing. For it was so that she called the part of the room in which the little bells were always ringing. "Won't it be nice to have 3*s.* 6*d.* instead of 3*s.*?" Lucy said solemnly that any increase of income was always nice, and that when such income was earned by superiority of acquirement it was a matter of just pride. This she enunciated with something of a dogmatic air; having schooled herself to give all due praise to Sophy, although it had to be given at the expense of her own feelings. But when Sophy said in reply that that was just what she had been thinking herself, and that as she could do her work by ear she was of course worth more than those who could not, then the other could only with difficulty repress the soreness of her heart.

But to Sophy I think the new arrangements were most pleasant because it enabled her to reach the street in which she lived just when Abraham Hall was accustomed to return from his work. He would generally come home,—to clean himself as she called it,—and would then again go out for his employment or amusement for the evening; and now, by a proper system of lying in wait, by creeping slow or walking quick, and by watching well, she was generally able to have a word or two with him. But he was so very bashful! He would always call her Miss Wilson; and she of course was obliged to call him Mr. Hall. "How is Miss Graham?" he asked one evening.

"She is very well. I think Lucy is always well. I never knew anybody so strong as she is."

"It is a great blessing. And how are you yourself?"

"I do get so tired at that nasty office. Though of course I like what I am doing now better than the other. It was that rolling up the bands that used to kill me. But I don't think I shall ever really be strong till I get away from the telegraphs. I suppose you have no young ladies where you are?"

"There are I believe a lot of them in the building, stitching bindings; but I never see them."

"I don't think you care much for young ladies, Mr. Hall."

"Not much—now."

"Why not now? What does that mean?"

"I dare say I never told you or Miss Graham before. But I had a wife of my own for a time."

"A wife! You!"

"Yes indeed. But she did not stay with me long. She left me before we had been a year married."

"Left you!"

"She died," he said, correcting very quickly the false impression which his words had been calculated to make.

"Dear me! Died before a year was out. How sad!"

"It was very sad."

"And you had no,—no,—no baby, Mr. Hall?"

"I wish she had had none, because then she would have been still living. Yes, I have a boy. Poor little mortal! It is two years old I think to-day."

"I should so like to see him. A little boy! Do bring him some day, Mr. Hall." Then the father explained that the child was in the country, down in Hertfordshire; but nevertheless he promised that he would some day bring him up to town and show him to his new friends.

Surely having once been married and having a child he must want another wife! And yet how little apt he was to say or do any of those things by saying and doing which men are supposed to express their desire in that direction! He was very slow at making love; —so slow that Sophy hardly found herself able to make use of her own little experiences with him. Alec Murray, who, however, in the way of a husband was not worth thinking of, had a great deal more to say for himself. She could put on her ribbons for Mr. Hall, and wait for him in the street, and look up into his face, and call him Mr. Hall;—but she could not tell him how dearly she would love that little boy and what an excellent mother she would be to him, unless he gave her some encouragement.

When Lucy heard that he had been a married man and that he had a child she was gratified, though she knew not why. "Yes, I should like to see him of course," she said, speaking of the boy. "A child, if you have not the responsibility of taking care of it, is always nice."

"I should so like to take care of it."

"I should not like to ask him to bring the boy up out of the country." She paused a moment, and then added, "He is just the man whom I should have thought would have married, and just the man to be made very serious by the grief of such a loss. I am coming to think it does a person good to have to bear troubles."

"You would not say that if you always felt as sick as I do after your day's work."

About a week after that Sophy was so weak in the middle of the day that she was obliged to leave the office and go home. "I know it will kill me," she said that evening, "if I go on with it. The place is so stuffy and nasty, and then those terrible stairs. If I could get out of it and settle down, then I should be quite well. I am not made for that kind of work;—not like you are."

"I think I was made for it certainly."

"It is such a blessing to be strong," said poor Sophy.

"Yes; it is a blessing. And I do bless God that he has made me so. It is the one good thing that has been given to me, and it is better, I think, than all the others." As she said this she looked at Sophy and thought that she was very pretty; but she thought also that prettiness had its dangers and its temptations; and that good strong serviceable health might perhaps be better for one who had to earn her bread.

But through all these thoughts there was a great struggle going on within her. To be able to earn one's bread without personal suffering is very good. To be tempted by prettiness to ribbons, pomatum, and vanities which one cannot afford is very bad. To do as Sophy was doing in regard to this young man, setting her cap at him and resolving to make prey of him as a fowler does of a bird, was, to her way of thinking, most unseemly. But to be loved by such a man as Abraham Hall, to be chosen by him as his companion, to be removed from the hard, outside, unwomanly work of the world to the indoor occupations which a husband would require from her; how much better a life according to her real tastes would that be, than anything which she now saw before her! It was all very well to be brown and strong while the exigencies of her position were those which now surrounded her; but she could not keep herself from dreaming of something which would have been much better than that.

A month or two passed away during which the child had on one occasion been brought up to town on a Saturday evening, and had been petted and washed and fed and generally cared for by the two girls during the Sunday,—all which greatly increased their intimacy with the father. And now, as Lucy quickly observed, Abraham Hall called Sophy by her christian name. When the word was first pronounced in Lucy's presence Sophy blushed and looked round at her friend. But she never said that the change had been made at her own request. "I do so hate to be called Miss Wilson," she had said. "It seems among friends as though I were a hundred years old." Then he had called her Sophy. But she did not dare,—not as yet, —to call him Abraham. All which the other girl watched very closely, saying nothing.

But during these two months Sophy had been away from her office more than half the time. Then the doctor said she had better leave town for awhile. It was September, and it was desired that she should pass that month at Hastings. Now it should be explained that in such emergencies as this the department has provided a most kindly aid for young women. Some five or six at a time are sent out for a month to Hastings or to Brighton, and are employed in the telegraph offices in those towns. Their railway fares are paid for them, and a small extra allowance is made to them to enable them to live away from their homes. The

privilege is too generally sought to be always at the
command of her who wants it; nor is it accorded ex-
cept on the doctor's certificate.   But in the September
Sophy Wilson was sent down to Hastings.

In spite, however, of the official benevolence which
greatly lightened the special burden which illness must
always bring on those who have to earn their bread,
and which in Sophy Wilson's case had done so much
for her, nevertheless the weight of the misfortune fell
heavily on poor Lucy.   Some little struggle had to be
made as to clothes before the girl could be sent away
from her home; and, though the sick one was enabled
to support herself at Hastings, the cost of the London
lodgings which should have been divided fell entirely
upon Lucy.   Then at the end of the month there came
worse tidings.   The doctor at Hastings declared that
the girl was unfit to go back to her work,—was, indeed, altogether unfit for such effort as eight hours'
continued attendance required from her.   She wanted
at any rate some period of perfect rest, and therefore
she remained down at the seaside without the extra
allowance which was so much needed for her maintenance.

Then the struggle became very severe with Lucy,
—so severe that she began to doubt whether she could
long endure it.   Sophy had her two shillings a day,
the two-thirds of her wages, but she could not subsist
on that.   Something had to be sent to her in addition,
and this something could only come from Lucy's wages.
So at least it was at first.   In order to avoid debt she
gave up her more comfortable room and went upstairs
into a little garret.   And she denied herself her accustomed dinner at the office, contenting herself with

bread and cheese,—or often simply with bread,—which she could take in her pocket. And she washed her own clothes and mended even her own boots, so that still she might send a part of her earnings to the sick one.

"Is she better?" Abraham asked her one day.

"It is hard to know, Mr. Hall. She writes just as she feels at the moment. I am afraid she fears to return to the office."

"Perhaps it does not suit her."

"I suppose not. She thinks some other kind of life would be better for her. I dare say it would."

"Could I do anything?" asked the man very slowly.

Could he do anything? well; yes. Lucy at least thought that he could do a great deal. There was one thing which, if he would do it, would make Sophy at any rate believe herself to be well. And this sickness was not organic,—was not, as it appeared, due to any cause which could be specified. It had not as yet been called by any name,—such as consumption. General debility had been spoken of both by the office doctor and by him at Hastings. Now Lucy certainly thought that a few words from Mr. Hall would do more than all the doctors in the way of effecting a cure. Sophy hated the telegraph office, and she lacked the strength of mind necessary for doing that which was distasteful to her. And that idea of a husband had taken such hold of her, that nothing else seemed to her to give a prospect of contentment. "Why don't you go down and see her, Mr. Hall?" she said.

Then he was silent for awhile before he answered, —silent and very thoughtful. And Lucy as the sound of her own words rested on her ears felt she had done wrong in asking such a question. Why should he go down, unless indeed he were in love with the girl and prepared to ask her to be his wife? If he were to go down expressly to visit her at Hastings unless he were so prepared, what false hopes he would raise; what damage he would do instead of good! How indeed could he possibly go down on such a mission without declaring to all the world that he intended to make the girl his wife? But it was necessary that the question should be answered. "I could do no good by that," he said.

"No; perhaps not. Only I thought——"

"What did you think?" Now he asked a question and showed plainly by his manner that he expected an answer.

"I don't know," said Lucy blushing. "I suppose I ought not to have thought anything. But you seemed to be so fond of her."

"Fond of her! Well; one does get fond of kind neighbours. I suppose you would think me impertinent, Miss Lucy,"—he had never made even this approach to familiarity before,—"if I were to say that I am fond of both of you."

"No indeed," she replied, thinking that as a fondness declared by a young man for two girls at one and the same moment could not be interesting, so neither could it be impertinent.

"I don't think I should do any good by going down. All that kind of thing costs so much money."

"Of course it does, and I was very wrong."

"But I should like to do something, Miss Lucy." And then he put his hand into his trousers pocket, and Lucy knew that he was going to bring forth money.

She was very poor; but the idea of taking money from him was shocking to her. According to her theory of life, even though Sophy had been engaged to the man as his promised wife, she should not consent to accept maintenance from him or pecuniary aid till she had been made, in very truth, flesh of his flesh, and bone of his bone. Presents an engaged girl might take of course, but hardly even presents of simple utility. A shawl might be given, so that it was a pretty thing and not a shawl merely for warmth. An engaged girl should rather live on bread and water up to her marriage, than take the means of living from the man she loved, till she could take it by right of having become his wife. Such were her feelings, and now she knew that this man was about to offer her money. "We shall do very well," she said, "Sophy and I together."

"You are very hard pinched," he replied. "You have given up your room."

"Yes, I have done that. When I was alone I did not want so big a place."

"I suppose I understand all about it," he said somewhat roughly, or, perhaps, gruffly would be the better word. "I think there is one thing poor people ought never to do. They ought never to be ashamed of being poor among themselves."

Then she looked up into his face, and as she did so a tear formed itself in each of her eyes. "Am I ashamed of anything before you?" she asked.

"You are afraid of telling the truth lest I should offer to help you. I know you don't have your dinner regular as you used."

"Who has dared to tell you that, Mr. Hall? What is my dinner to anybody?"

18*

"Well. It is something to me. If we are to be friends of course I don't like seeing you go without your meals. You'll be ill next yourself."

"I am very strong."

"It isn't the way to keep so, to work without the victuals you're used to." He was talking to her now in such a tone as to make her almost feel that he was scolding her. "No good can come of that. You are sending your money down to Hastings to her."

"Of course we share everything."

"You wouldn't take anything from me for yourself I dare say. Anybody can see how proud you are. But if I leave it for her I don't think you have a right to refuse it. Of course she wants it if you don't." With that he brought out a sovereign and put it down on the table.

"Indeed I couldn't, Mr. Hall," she said.

"I may give it to her if I please."

"You can send it her yourself," said Lucy, not knowing how else to answer him.

"No, I couldn't. I don't know her address." Then without waiting for another word he walked out of the room, leaving the sovereign on the table. This occurred in a small back parlour on the ground floor, which was in the occupation of the landlady, but was used sometimes by the lodgers for such occasional meetings.

What was she to do with the sovereign? She would be very angry if any man were to send her a sovereign; but it was not right that she should measure Sophy's feelings by her own. And then it might still be that the man was sending the present to the girl whom he intended to make his wife. But why—why

—why, had he asked about her dinner? What were her affairs to him? Would she not have gone without her dinner for ever rather than have taken it at his hands? And yet, who was there in all the world of whom she thought so well as of him? And so she took the sovereign upstairs with her into her garret.

CHAPTER IV.

MR. BROWN THE HAIRDRESSER.

LUCY, when she got up to her own little room with the sovereign, sat for awhile on the bed, crying. But she could not in the least explain to herself why it was that she was shedding tears at this moment. It was not because Sophy was ill, though that was cause to her of great grief; nor because she herself was so hard put to it for money to meet her wants. It may be doubted whether grief or pain ever does of itself produce tears, which are rather the outcome of some emotional feeling. She was not thinking much of Sophy as she cried, nor certainly were her own wants present to her mind. The sovereign was between her fingers, but she did not at first even turn her mind to that, or consider what had best be done with it. But what right had he to make inquiry as to her poverty? It was that, she told herself, which now provoked her to anger so that she wept from sheer vexation. Why should he have searched into her wants and spoken to her of her need of victuals? What had there been between them to justify him in tearing away that veil of custom which is always supposed to hide our private necessities from our acquaintances till we ourselves feel

called upon to declare them? He had talked to her
about her meals. He ought to know that she would
starve rather than accept one from him. Yes;—she
was very angry with him, and would henceforth keep
herself aloof from him.

But still, as she sat, there were present to her eyes
and ears the form and words of a heroic man. He
had seemed to scold her; but there are female hearts
which can be better reached and more surely touched
by the truth of anger than by the patent falseness of
flattery. Had he paid her compliments she would not
now have been crying, nor would she have complained
to herself of his usage; but she certainly would not
have sat thinking of him, wondering what sort of
woman had been that young wife to whom he had first
given himself, wondering whether it was possible that
Sophy should be good enough for him.

Then she got up, and looking down upon her own
hand gazed at the sovereign till she had made up her
mind what she would do with it. She at once sat
down and wrote to Sophy. She had made up her
mind. There should be no diminution in the contribution made from her own wages. In no way should
any portion of that sovereign administer to her own
comfort. Though she might want her accustomed
victuals ever so badly, they should not come to her
from his earnings. So she told Sophy in the letter
that Mr. Hall had expressed great anxiety for her welfare, and had begged that she would accept a present
from him. She was to get anything with the sovereign
that might best tend to her happiness. But the shilling
a day which Lucy contributed out of her own wages
was sent with the sovereign.

For an entire month she did not see Abraham Hall again so as to do more than just speak to him on the stairs. She was almost inclined to think that he was cold and unkind in not seeking her;—and yet she wilfully kept out of his way. On each Sunday it would at any rate have been easy for her to meet him; but with a stubborn purpose which she did not herself understand she kept herself apart, and when she met him on the stairs, which she would do occasionally when she returned from her work, she would hardly stand till she had answered his inquiries after Sophy. But at the end of the month one evening he came up and knocked at her door. "I am sorry to intrude, Miss Lucy."

"It is no intrusion, Mr. Hall. I wish I had a place to ask you to sit down in."

"I have come to bring another trifle for Miss Sophy."

"Pray do not do it. I cannot send it her. She ought not to take it. I am sure you know that she ought not to take it."

"I know nothing of the kind. If I know anything, it is that the strong should help the weak, and the healthy the sick. Why should she not take it from me as well as from you?"

It was necessary that Lucy should think a little before she could answer this;—but, when she had thought, her answer was ready, "We are both girls."

"Is there anything which ought to confine kindness to this or the other sex? If you were knocked down in the street would you let no one but a woman pick you up?"

"It is not the same. I know you understand it, Mr. Hall. I am sure you do."

Then he also paused to think what he would say, for he was conscious that he did "understand it." For a young woman to accept money from a man seemed to imply that some return of favours would be due. But,—he said to himself,—that feeling came from what was dirty and not from what was noble in the world. "You ought to lift yourself above all that," he said at last. "Yes; you ought. You are very good, but you would be better if you would do so. You say that I understand, and I think that you, too, understand." This again was said in that voice which seemed to scold, and again her eyes became full of tears. Then he was softer on a sudden. "Good night, Miss Lucy. You will shake hands with me;—will you not?" She put her hand in his, being perfectly conscious at the moment that it was the first time that she had ever done so. What a mighty hand it seemed to be as it held hers for a moment! "I will put the sovereign on the table," he said, again leaving the room and giving her no option as to its acceptance.

But she made up her mind at once that she would not be the means of sending his money to Sophy Wilson. She was sure that she would take nothing from him for her own relief, and therefore sure that neither ought Sophy to do so,—at any rate unless there had been more between them than either of them had told to her. But Sophy must judge for herself. She sent, therefore, the sovereign back to Hall with a little note as follows:—

"Dear Mr. Hall,—Sophy's address is at
    "Mrs. Pike's,
        "19, Paradise Row,
            "Fairlight, near Hastings.
"You can do as you like as to writing to her. I
am obliged to send back the money which you have
so *very generously* left for her, because I do not think
she ought to accept it. If she were quite in want it
might be different, but we have still five shillings a
day between us. If a young woman were starving
perhaps it ought to be the same as though she were
being run over in the street, but it is not like that. In
my next letter I shall tell Sophy all about it.
                    "Yours truly,
                        "Lucy Graham."

The following evening, when she came home, he
was standing at the house door evidently waiting for
her. She had never seen him loitering in that way
before, and she was sure that he was there in order
that he might speak to her.

"I thought I would let you know that I got the
sovereign safely," he said. "I am so sorry that you
should have returned it."

"I am sure that I was right, Mr. Hall."

"There are cases in which it is very hard to say
what is right and what is wrong. Some things seem
right because people have been wrong so long. To
give and take among friends ought to be right."

"We can only do what we think right," she said,
as she passed in through the passage upstairs.

She felt sure from what had passed that he had
not sent the money to Sophy. But why not? Sophy

had said that he was bashful. Was he so far bashful
that he did not dare himself to send the money to the
girl he loved, though he had no scruple as to giving it
to her through another person? And, as for bashful-
ness, it seemed to her that the man spoke out his mind
clearly enough. He could scold her, she thought, without any difficulty, for it still seemed that his voice and
manner were rough to her. He was never rough to
Sophy; but then she had heard so often that love will
alter a man amazingly!

Then she wrote her letter to Sophy, and explained
as well as she could the whole affair. She was quite
sure that Sophy would regret the loss of the money.
Sophy, she knew, would have accepted it without
scruple. People, she said to herself, will be different.
But she endeavoured to make her friend understand
that she, with her feelings, could not be the medium
of sending on presents of which she disapproved. "I
have given him your address," she said, "and he can
suit himself as to writing to you." In this letter she
enclosed a money order for the contribution made to
Sophy's comfort out of her own wages.

Sophy's answer, which came in a day or two, surprised her very much. "As to Mr. Hall's money," she
began, "as things stand at present perhaps it is as well
that you didn't take it." As Lucy had expected that
grievous fault would be found with her, this was comfortable. But it was after that, that the real news
came. Sophy was a great deal better; that was also
good tidings;—but she did not want to leave Hastings
just at present. Indeed she thought that she did not
want to leave it at all. A very gentlemanlike young
man, who was just going to be taken into partnership

in a hairdressing establishment, had proposed to her;
—and she had accepted him. Then there were two
wishes expressed;—the first was that Lucy would go
on a little longer with her kind generosity, and the
second,—that Mr. Hall would not feel it very much.

As regarded the first wish, Lucy resolved that she
would go on at least for the present. Sophy was still
on sick leave from the office, and, even though she
might be engaged to a hairdresser, was still to be regarded as an invalid. But as to Mr. Hall, she thought
that she could do nothing. She could not even tell
him,—at any rate till that marriage at Hastings was
quite a settled thing. But she thought that Mr. Hall's
future happiness would not be lessened by the event.
Though she had taught herself to love Sophy, she had
been unable not to think that her friend was not a
fitting wife for such a man. But in telling herself that
he would have an escape, she put it to herself as
though the fault lay chiefly in him. "He is so stern
and so hard that he would have crushed her, and she
never would have understood his justness and honesty."
In her letter of congratulation, which was very kind,
she said not a word of Abraham Hall, but she promised to go on with her own contribution till things
were a little more settled.

In the meantime she was very poor. Even brown
dresses won't wear for ever, let them be ever so brown,
and in the first flurry of sending Sophy off to Hastings,
—with that decent apparel which had perhaps been
the means of winning the hairdresser's heart,—she had
got somewhat into debt with her landlady. This she
was gradually paying off, even on her reduced wages,

but the effort pinched her closely. Day by day, in spite of all her efforts with her needle, she became sensible of a deterioration in her outward appearance which was painful to her at the office, and which made her most careful to avoid any meeting with Abraham Hall. Her boots were very bad, and she had now for some time given up even the pretence of gloves as she went backwards and forwards to the office. But perhaps it was her hat that was most vexatious. The brown straw hat which had lasted her all the summer and autumn could hardly be induced to keep its shape now when November was come.

One day, about three o'clock in the afternoon, Abraham Hall went to the Post Office, and, having inquired among the messengers, made his way up to the telegraph department at the top of the building. There he asked for Miss Graham, and was told by the doorkeeper that the young ladies were not allowed to receive visitors during office hours. He persisted, however, explaining that he had no wish to go into the room, but that it was a matter of importance, and that he was very anxious that Miss Graham should be asked to come out to him. Now it is a rule that the staff of the department who are engaged in sending and receiving messages, the privacy of which may be of vital importance, should be kept during the hours of work as free as possible from communication with the public. It is not that either the girls or the young men would be prone to tell the words which they had been the means of passing on to their destination, but that it might be worth the while of some sinner to offer great temptation, and that the power of offering it should be lessened as much as possible. Therefore, when Abraham Hall pressed his request the door-keeper told him that it was quite impossible.

"Do you mean to say that if it were an affair of life and death she could not be called out?" Abraham asked in that voice which had sometimes seemed to Lucy to be so impressive. "She is not a prisoner!"

"I don't know as to that," replied the man; "you would have to see the superintendent, I suppose."

"Then let me see the superintendent." And at last he did succeed in seeing some one whom he so convinced of the importance of his message as to bring Lucy to the door.

"Miss Graham," he said, when they were at the top of the stairs, and so far alone that no one else could hear him, "I want you to come out with me for half an hour."

"I don't think I can. They won't let me."

"Yes they will. I have to say something which I must say now."

"Will not the evening do, Mr. Hall?"

"No; I must go out of town by the mail train from Paddington, and it will be too late. Get your hat and come with me for half an hour."

Then she remembered her hat, and she snatched a glance at her poor stained dress, and she looked up at him. He was not dressed in his working clothes, and his face and hands were clean, and altogether there was a look about him of well-to-do manly tidiness which added to her feeling of shame.

"If you will go on to the house I will follow you," she said.

"Are you ashamed to walk with me?"

"I am, because——"

He had not understood her at first, but now he understood it all. "Get your hat," he said, "and come with a friend who is really a friend. You must come; you must, indeed." Then she felt herself compelled to obey, and went back and got her old hat and followed him down the stairs into the street. "And so Miss Wilson is going to be married," were the first words he said in the street.

"Has she written to you?"

"Yes; she has told me all about it. I am so glad that she should be settled to her liking, out of town. She says that she is nearly well now. I hope that Mr. Brown is a good sort of man, and that he will be kind to her."

It could hardly be possible, Lucy thought, that he should have taken her away from the office merely to talk to her of Sophy's prospects. It was evident that he was strong enough to conceal any chagrin which might have been caused by Sophy's apostacy. Could it, however, be the case that he was going to leave London because his feelings had been too much disturbed to allow of his remaining quiet? "And so you are going away? Is it for long?" "Well, yes; I suppose it is for always." Then there came upon her a sense of increased desolation. Was he not her only friend? And then, though she had refused all pecuniary assistance, there had been present to her a feeling that there was near to her a strong human being whom she could trust, and who in any last extremity could be kind to her.

"For always! And you go to-night!" Then she thought that he had been right to insist on seeing her.

It would certainly have been a great blow to her if he had gone without a word of farewell.

"There is a man wanted immediately to look after the engines at a great establishment on the Wye, in the Forest of Dean. They have offered me four pounds a week."

"Four pounds a week!"

"But I must go at once. It has been talked about for some time, and now it has come all in a clap. I have to be off without a day's notice, almost before I know where I am. As for leaving London, it is just what I like. I love the country."

"Oh, yes," said Lucy, "that will be nice;—and about your little boy?" Could it be that she was to be asked to do something for the child?

They were now at the door of their house.

"Here we are," he said, "and perhaps I can say better inside what I have got to say." Then she followed him into the back sitting-room on the ground floor.

CHAPTER V.
ABRAHAM HALL MARRIED.

"Yes;" he said;—"about my little boy. I could not say what I had to say in the street, though I had thought to do so." Then he paused, and she sat herself down, feeling, she did not know why, as though she would lack strength to hear him if she stood. It was then the case that some particular service was to be demanded from her,—something that would show his confidence in her. The very idea of this seemed

at once to add a grace to her life. She would have
the child to love. There would be something for her
to do. And there must be letters between her and
him. It would certainly add a grace to her life. But
how odd that he should not take his child with him!
He had paused a moment while she thought of all this,
and she was aware that he was looking at her. But
she did not dare to return his gaze, or even to glance
up at his face. And then gradually she felt that she
was shivering and trembling. What was it that ailed
her,—just now when it would be so necessary that she
should speak out with some strength? She had eaten
nothing since her breakfast when he had come to her,
and she was afraid that she would show herself to be
weak. "Will you be his mother?" he said.

What did it mean? How was she to answer him?
She knew that his eyes were on her, but hers were
more than ever firmly fixed upon the floor. And she
was aware that she ought briskly to have acceded to
his request,—so as to have shown by her ready alacrity
that she had attributed no other meaning to the words
than they had been intended to convey,—that she had
not for a moment been guilty of rash folly. But though
it was so imperative upon her to say a word, yet she
could not speak. Everything was swimming round her.
She was not even sure that she could sit upon her
chair. "Lucy," he said;—then she thought she would
have fallen;—"Lucy, will you be my wife?"

There was no doubt about the word. Her sense
of hearing was at any rate not deficient. And there
came upon her at once a thorough conviction that all
her troubles had been changed for ever and a day into
joys and blessings. The word had been spoken from

which he certainly would never go back, and which of course,—of course,—must be a commandment to her. But yet there was an unfitness about it which disturbed her, and she was still powerless to speak. The remembrance of the meanness of her clothes and poorness of her position came upon her,—so that it would be her duty to tell him that she was not fit for him; and yet she could not speak.

"If you will say that you want time to think about it, I shall be contented," he said. But she did not want a moment to think about it. She could not have confessed to herself that she had learned to love him, —oh, so much too dearly,—if it were not for this most unexpected, most unthought of, almost impossible revelation. But she did not want a moment to make herself sure that she did love him. Yet she could not speak. "Will you say that you will think of it for a month?"

Then there came upon her an idea that he was not asking this because he loved her, but in order that he might have a mother whom he could trust for his child. Even that would have been flattering, but that would not have sufficed. Then when she told herself what she was, or rather what she thought herself to be, she felt sure that he could not really love her. Why should such a man as he love such a woman? Then her mouth was opened. "You cannot want me for myself," she said.

"Not for yourself! Then why? I am not the man to seek any girl for her fortune, and you have none." Then again she was dumbfounded. She could not explain what she meant. She could not say,—because I am brown, and because I am plain, and because I have become thin and worn from want, and because my clothes are old and shabby. "I ask you," he said, "because with all my heart I love you."

It was as though the heavens had been opened to her. That he should speak a word that was not true was to her impossible. And, as it was so, she would not coy her love to him for a moment. If only she could have found words with which to speak to him! She could not even look up at him, but she put out her hand so as to touch him. "Lucy," he said, "stand up and come to me." Then she stood up and with one little step crept close to his side. "Lucy, can you love me?" And as he asked the question his arm was pressed round her waist, and as she put up her hand to welcome rather than to restrain his embrace, she again felt the strength, the support, and the warmth of his grasp. "Will you not say that you love me?"

"I am such a poor thing," she replied.

"A poor thing, are you? Well, yes; there are different ways of being poor. I have been poor enough in my time, but I never thought myself a poor thing. And you must not say it ever of yourself again."

"No?"

"My girl must not think herself a poor thing. May I not say, my girl?" Then there was just a little murmur, a sound which would have been "yes" but for the inability of her lips to open themselves. "And if my girl, then my wife. And shall my wife be called a poor thing? No, Lucy. I have seen it all. I don't think I like poor things;—but I like you."

"Do you?"

"I do. And now I must go back to the City Road and give up charge and take my money. And I must leave this at seven—after a cup of tea. Shall I see you again?"

"See me again! Oh, to-day, you mean. Indeed you shall. Not see you off? My own, own, own man?"

"What will they say at the office?"

"I don't care what they say. Let them say what they like. I have never been absent a day yet without leave. What time shall I be here?" Then he named an hour. "Of course I will have your last words. Perhaps you will tell me something that I must do."

"I must leave some money with you."

"No; no; no; not yet. That shall come after." This she said smiling up at him, with a sparkle of a tear in each eye, but with such a smile! Then he caught her in his arms and kissed her. "That may come at present at any rate," he said. To this, though it was repeated once and again, there was no opposition. Then in his own masterful manner he put on his hat and stalked out of the room without any more words.

She must return to the office that afternoon, of course, if only for the sake of explaining her wish to absent herself the rest of the day. But she could not go forth into the streets just yet. Though she had been able to smile at him and to return his caress, and for a moment so to stand by him that she might have something of the delight of his love, still she was too much flurried, too weak from the excitement of the last half-hour, to walk back to the Post Office without allowing herself some minutes to recruit her strength and collect her thoughts. She went at once up to her own room and cut for herself a bit of bread which she began to eat,—just as one would trim one's lamp carefully for some night work, even though oppressed by heaviest sorrow, or put fuel on the fire that would be needed. Then having fed herself, she leaned back in her chair, throwing her handkerchief over her face, in order that she might think of it.

Oh,—how much there was to fill her mind with many thoughts! Looking back to what she had been even an hour ago, and then assuring herself with infinite delight of the certain happiness of her present position, she told herself that all the world had been altered to her within that short space. As for loving him;—there was no doubt about that! Now she could own to herself that she had long since loved him, even when she thought that he might probably take that other girl as his wife. That she should love him, —was it not a matter of course, he being what he was? But that he should love her,—that, that was the marvel! But he did. She need not doubt that. She could remember distinctly each word of assurance that he had spoken to her. "I ask you, because with all my heart I love you." "May I not say my girl;— and, if my girl, then my wife?" "I do not think that. I like poor things; but I like you." No. If she were regarded by him as good enough to be his wife then she would certainly never call herself a poor thing again.

In her troubles and her poverty,—especially in her solitude, she had often thought of that other older man who had wanted to make her his wife,—sometimes almost with regret. There would have been duties for her and a home, and a mode of life more fitting to her feminine nature than this solitary tedious existence. And there would have been something for her to love, some human being on whom to spend her human solicitude and sympathies. She had leagued herself with Sophy Wilson, and she had been true to the bond; but it had had in it but little satisfaction. The other life, she had sometimes thought, would have been better. But she had never loved the man, and could not have loved him as a husband should, she thought, be loved by his wife. She had done what was right in refusing the good things which he had offered her,—and now she was rewarded! Now had come to her the bliss of which she had dreamed, that of belonging to a man to whom she felt that she was bound by all the chords of her heart. Then she repeated his name to herself,—Abraham Hall, and tried in a lowest whisper the sound of that other name,— Lucy Hall. And she opened her arms wide as she sat upon the chair as though in that way she could take his child to her bosom.

She had been sitting so nearly an hour when she started up suddenly and again put on her old hat and hurried off towards her office. She felt now that as regarded her clothes she did not care about herself. There was a paradise prepared for her so dear and so near that the present was made quite bright by merely being the short path to such a future. But for his sake she cared. As belonging to him she would fain, had it been possible, not have shown herself in a garb unfitting for his wife. Everything about him had always been decent, fitting, and serviceable! Well! It was his own doing. He had chosen her as she was.

She would not run in debt to make herself fit for his notice, because such debts would have been debts to be paid by him. But if she could squeeze from her food what should supply her with garments fit at any rate to stand with him at the altar it should be done.

Then, as she hurried on to the office, she remembered what he had said about money. No! She would not have his money till it was hers of right. Then with what perfect satisfaction would she take from him whatever he pleased to give her, and how hard would she work for him in order that he might never feel that he had given her his good things for nothing!

It was five o'clock before she was at the office, and she had promised to be back in the lodgings at six, to get for him his tea. It was quite out of the question that she should work to-day. "The truth is, ma'am," she said to the female superintendent, "I have received and accepted an offer of marriage this afternoon. He is going out of town to-night, and I want to be with him before he goes." This is a plea against which official rigour cannot prevail. I remember once when a young man applied to a saturnine pundit who ruled matters in a certain office for leave of absence for a month to get married. "To get married!" said the saturnine pundit. "Poor fellow! But you must have the leave." The lady at the telegraph office was no doubt less caustic, and dismissed our Lucy for the day with congratulations rather than pity.

She was back at the lodging before her lover, and had borrowed the little back parlour from Mrs. Green, and had spread the tea-things, and herself made the toast in the kitchen before he came. "There's something I suppose more nor friendship betwixt you and Mr. Hall, and better," said the landlady smiling. "A great deal better, Mrs. Green," Lucy had replied, with her face intent upon the toast. "I thought it never could have been that other young lady," said Mrs. Green.

"And now, my dear, about money," said Abraham as he rose to prepare himself for the journey. Many things had been settled over that meal,—how he was to get a house ready, and was then to say when she should come to him, and how she should bring the boy with her, and how he would have the banns called in the church, and how they would be married as soon as possible after her arrival in the new country. "And now, my dear, about money?"

She had to take it at last. "Yes," she said, "it is right that I should have things fit to come to you in. It is right that you shouldn't be disgraced."

"I'd marry you in a sack from the poor-house, if it were necessary," he said with vehemence.

"As it is not necessary, it shall not be so. I will get things;—but they shall belong to you always; and I will not wear them till the day that I also shall belong to you."

She went with him that night to the station, and kissed him openly as she parted from him on the platform. There was nothing in her love now of which she was ashamed. How, after some necessary interval, she followed him down into Gloucestershire, and how she became his wife standing opposite to him in the bright raiment which his liberality had supplied, and how she became as good a wife as ever blessed a man's household, need hardly here be told.

That Miss Wilson recovered her health and married the hairdresser may be accepted by all anxious readers as an undoubted fact.

THE END.

PRINTING OFFICE OF THE PUBLISHER.

This is the end of this publication.

Any remaining blank pages are for our book binding requirements and are blank on purpose.

To search thousands of interesting publications like this one, please remember to visit our website at:

http://www.kessinger.net

Printed in the United States
45559LVS00004B/7

9 781425 475758